TIMED

HOW TO SPEND YOUR TIME

RIGHT; BETTER START LATE THAN NEVER

VICTORIA ADESANYA

ACKNOWLEDGEMENTS

Firstly, I would like to give all the accolade to the one who has brought this book to reality - God almighty for the grace to write this book.

I'd like to say a thank you to

Babs Adesanya,

Who shares his thoughts with me daily

My Family,

Who, one way or the other contributed to the experiences I shared in this book, and

Feji Khai,

A childhood pen pal now editor who proofread and edited the manuscript.

FOREWORD

TIME is the dynamic currency of life. It is a universal period between life and death and an incredible measure of destiny. The creation analysis in Gen. 1.1 indicates that God, the timeless Timer, programmed the account of creation as a framework of Time. The word "In the beginning" connotes "Time". Here we see the first mention of 'GOD' within a time frame. Gen. 1.1 "In the beginning, God created the heavens and the earth. 2 and the earth was without form (shapelessness); and void (emptiness); and darkness was upon the face of the deep (thick darkness). And the Spirit of God moved upon the face of the waters. God's systematic approach to creation gloriously manifested here. There was a 'Time' the heavens and the earth were created; there was a 'Time' when shapelessness, emptiness and darkness prevailed over the earth, and there was a time when the creative power of God commanded 'Light' to appear and it was so. (Gen. 1:3) Before light came, the ancient weapon of mass distraction – shapelessness, emptiness and darkness, reigned supreme over the whole earth because that was their time.

The moment light came, darkness disappeared at the speed of light, in a moment, within a twinkle of an eye, the period of darkness became history while a brand-new world emerged within six days.

Right from the beginning we have seen there is a 'Time' for everything and a season for every activity under heaven (Eccl. 3:1 NIV). Between 'A time to be born' and 'A time to die' lies various seasons of growth, the pursuit of purpose, seasons of empowerment, exploits, challenges, opportunities and setbacks. Everyone is timed to go through these periods in our lifetime. As each day passes by, you are a step closer to the grave.
The Almighty God framed us mankind made in his image and likeness in three segments of life-time. The morning season that is, from infancy to adolescence;

the afternoon and the evening session. Let's now see the life of Moses as a typical example here. He spent one hundred and twenty years on earth, divided into three segments. The first forty years Moses was learning to be everything; the second forty years he learned to be nothing. Here he was being prepared for the assignment ahead, his Egyptian ego was broken down and replaced with a Shepherd's heart, fortified with Holy Spirit and Power; while in the third forty years of his life, Moses learned and understood that God is everything.

This and many other facts of life are widely discussed and extensively illustrated in this all-important book "TIMED". Having gone through this 'Time-tested truth', I discovered incredible concept and principles of Time Management, an application of which will create for the reader, a paradise of tremendous achievement.

Lastly, as important and universal as Time is, it has no permanent friend. If you handle it well, it is a worthwhile investment that can yield you great wealth. Understanding time will make you strike the iron while it is hot and make hay while the sun shines. I see 'Life-Time' as an Ice Cream – enjoy it before it melts! Get this book, don't just read it, study it and learn how to use your time wisely. Invest in yourself and experience comfort on every side. It's a matter of time.

REV. (DR.) EBENEZER AJITENA

TABLE OF CONTENT

INTRODUCTION

CHAPTER ONE - THE PURSUIT

CHAPTER TWO – THE BATTLE

CHAPTER THREE – KNOW YOUR PERSONAL MISSION STATEMENT

CHAPTER FIVE - REALISATION

Introduction

On the morning of 29th April 2018, I got to a major turning point in my life as I heard the voice say to me 'just start and I will back you up'. He spoke to me in that minute and now I am sure it was HIM.

I got really scared, I'm not even sure why. I haven't started anything yet, or not so much anyway. Why am I feeling this way? I had both a feeling of excitement and fear surging through me right at the same time. I knew whatever it was I was about to get myself into, was going to be fulfilling, yet I shrilled at the thought of it. Where do I start? How do I start? Who will help me? Can I even do it? I have a lot on my plate already!

All these thoughts overwhelmed my mind. Yet, I was certain it was the right thing to do. My inconsistencies and flaws almost stopped me from seeing my dream become a reality. In retrospective, I now know indeed, it doesn't matter how you feel, actions give birth to results and results are time-bound. Time is short and is of utmost value, whatever it is that scares you, is the exact thing you should venture into, and you will soon realise the result is well worth it.

The fact that this book is a reality, proves 'time' packed with actions in line with your goal, will give you that result you desire. I have picked up writing this book several times only to drop it, but Today! I am glad you are reading it.

One thing that made this book a reality is discipline. An action based decision to launch this book on a fixed date.

Pursuit- I began to work towards it,

Battle- Self motivation to keep writing

Realisation- told people about it that I could be accountable to.

The day it all started

It was just like any other normal day. I woke, and he spoke to me about going into children's ministry. It dawned on me then that a journey was beginning, a new phase of my life. I figured that it would translate to having to dedicatedly give this ministry whatever it takes. If it meant getting up in the wee hour to write whatever I'm shown.

At that point, it felt as if He was talking to me about the curriculum but then again I perceived that it probably was a self-development process. That resonated with me, because I am a big advocate of enjoying the process.

Are you scared of starting a journey or process, yet the thought of it just would not go away? I indulge you to start somehow, whichever way you have the capacity to now, start anyway, it's not too late to start! And it doent have to be perfect either, remember, *You are timed*.

On the 1st of May, 2018, I woke with a strange feeling. At first, I thought I understood the feeling, yes, I thought it was just a lazy feeling of not wanting to do anything. So, I battled in bed with getting up to prepare for work. I even thought of not turning up at work. 'They will struggle without me', I thought, 'Maybe I will feel better once I get to work and get on with my daily routine', but no, I could not shift the thought or the feelings that came with it. I got up in the end after numerous thoughts. After attending to my family, the thoughts returned to me and I decided to just flow with it.

I spent a few minutes sorting out some bills that I usually dealt with on the 1st of every month. In the process, I realised that I needed to find out more about the word 'CLARION' and have a better understanding of it. The word had lingered in my mind for so long and was what this whole process was about. Now, I am finally putting the dots together and getting the real message. The CLARION call!

Clarion

Cambridge English dictionary describes clarion as 'as a truly clear message or instruction about what action is needed'

Collins described it as '...to proclaim loudly, from medieval Latin clarion trumpet, meaning clear.'

But what caught my attention was from Vocabulary.com which says 'Clarion means loud and clear, and a clarion call is *a call to something hard to ignore*. Hard to ignore but also pure and clear in tone. There is nothing shrill or low about a clarion call.'

This definition shook me on many levels. It was just what I needed to hear about this call, which by the way I already knew. It was not intrusive in any way. It was not a call to something new, yet I struggled with following this amazingly simple, clear, and pure tone of instruction. I was happy to be finally embracing the call. I decided I would allow it to lead me to the world I was not yet familiar with but that I needed desperately to tread in.

Purpose

I believe 'purpose' has a lot to do with answering a clarion call.

'Purpose' is a word related in meaning to 'goal', 'meaning' and other words. 'Purpose' can be described as the kind of goals that affect and influence the lives of people other than oneself, which has the power to potentially change lives for the better.

One of such things might be a discovery of the vaccine for coronavirus, a launch of a new organisation, a research breakthrough on a subject matter or any noble venture. It is developed over years and can be quicker to ascertain in some individuals than others. These are some of the factors we discuss in this book. I use the word 'call' interchangeably with purpose. Your purpose is like a mandate, a requirement and the reason for existence. Your purpose can be broken down into meaningful goals that develop and evolve throughout your live. It definitely cannot be fully achieved in a month, a year, or even five years. It most likely is a lifetime call to service and impact.

I'm not helping if that sounds scary, but what this book will do is break this big elephant into small chunks to address it one segment at a time, simple enough for you to begin to put the big picture together and envision your dream, and see the world you are about to create.

In research by Leslie Francis, a link of sense of purpose amongst teenagers with the reading of the bible was carried out. A research of over 26,000 13 to 15-year olds in England and Wales showed that those who read their bible had a more prevalent sense of purpose than those who did not.

Having a sense of community and not isolation fosters this knowing and sense of responsibility to others and a group. Also reading inspirational and motivational materials can foster this sense of community. As you take on the role of many and enter into the different characters without necessarily having lived that path yourself. Seeing purpose in the life of others can help to foster it in your own life because it becomes a picture that you work within your mind.

Another great way to look at 'purpose' is that it is an experience that helps an individual instigate his or her critical thinking ability. So, if you are a parent, I will suggest that you share with your young children/adolescent now and again, how raising them has created a sense of purpose for you as a Mum or Dad. How your role at work helps and makes people's lives better and gives you the drive to rise in the morning to contribute to the world we live in.

Another area that helps to construct this meaning in life is through the pain you have been subjected to in life, and the pain of others, even that can spark a sense of purpose in a person. So, pain is not always a bad thing, but the outcome of it will determine whether it is good or bad.

In my own life, for example, I lived my teenage years with a head full of hair and a thick curly afro kinky hair. However, not long after having my children, this hair began to fall off and I ended up with thin, unhealthy, and severely broken hair. Some of you might not be able to relate to this, but this affected my self-esteem extremely, where I could not wear my hair confidently. But guess what, it gave birth to purpose - an evolving business with two stems- customised wig making services and hair coaching.

Another of such experiences was in 2005, when I had my first babies, as a 23-year-old. I had just finished university, got married, to the most handsome and tolerant man in the world. We had twins… gosh how excited we were. But then I lost one of my babies, yes. People who knew me then would know about this. It was a huge blow to take as a young lady with great dreams and a bright future ahead of her, yet it transformed my life.

I became so passionate about the early years of children that formed the course of my career for the next 12 years of my life. I studied 'early years' and went on to senior leadership in that field. This is the core of my life, as raising extraordinary children has become my passion and purpose.

So what am I saying, if you are thinking 'I don't know what my purpose is', 'I haven't had landmark moments like you have Victoria', why not write a list of the areas of pain you have experienced or are drawn to. You can also write the aspect of that movie or book that sticks out to you. You can also go to the library, online or a bookstore and begin to read about topics relating to what you have written down. I can assure you that as you do these, you will find your purpose in the process and begin to identify what matters to you.

The fundamental thing that determines whether your pain will crush or make you is character. We will focus on these characters later on in this book.

So in other to ensure your purpose is known and fulfilled in your *Timed* life, You need to ensure you spending time on the right things.

Chapter One
The Pursuit

Have you ever pursued something or have you ever been pursued by something?

I think of how a lion chases after a prey. This is a pursuit indeed!

A pursuit suggests that there are intentional actions taken or followed to achieve something. Pay attention to the word 'intentional' because nothing will happen of its own volition. Like the lion and its prey, the lion intentionally pursues. Even though he is strong and the king of the animal kingdom, he still intentionally pursues.

Intentionality is key here and not convenience or volition. Even when you talk of being spontaneous and sporadic, there always is an underlying belief or knowledge base that causes spontaneity. For example, you are a product of a sociological environment and whether consciously or unconsciously, you are fed certain opinions through your eye-gate or ear-gate, which your brain processes and uses at will. What I'm trying to say is this, as you begin the pursuit, there is every need to streamline your value, identify what thread or line you want to follow. As you systematically investigate and derive more knowledge, you will need to streamline it to achieve the desired outcome.

I remember another instance when I woke up with a strong determination to make the day count and so I began a listen within. Yes, doing a soul search. I had to intentionally make my environment conducive for me to introspect effectively. I didn't want any interruptions so I muted my phone, I didn't turn it off because I have responsibilities to cater to.

Then, I engaged in some time of meditation (worship to be precise) and when I was done, I sat still to pay attention to my thoughts.

And yes, I also fasted- this is the act of depriving oneself of the desire to eat or in some cases abstaining from an act or habit. This kind of time-out provides a great source of clarity. My intention in creating this environment was to FOCUS. What I discovered was exhilarating, I began to think of the various times I had been at this point and why things never changed. I was never intentional enough and did not possess the values to forge through or make strides.

Value

Don't be a wandering generality but be a meaningful specific.

Zig Ziglar

The more I made stride, the more I realised my shortcomings and inadequacy, and that in itself is a success, especially if I am not beating myself up for it. There is no need to be distressed over spilt milk. Look up, encourage yourself and move on!

I remember the story of David in the bible. He had fought, conquered, was merry and sang with the blokes, only to return home to meet with disaster just after a major win. Take a moment to imagine this. This is the part where most people break into swearing and lamenting, but not David, He encouraged himself in the Lord and went on to achieve greater feats.

In this journey of pursuit, there is every tendency to feel dejected and low but you must remember the values you develop- Perseverance, positive talk (not what you feel), endurance, are instrumental to the outcome you experience from this situation. Maintaining a state of composure is creative ability.

It is easy to simply, conform to the way you ought to react. However, daring to stand out causes a creativity chain effect. Aristotle, a Socratic, is credited for setting the foundation for modern science as we see it today. He dared to do something different. It was very scary but possible. Socrates, a great Athenian philosopher, had a motto *'Know Thyself.'*

Knowing Yourself

Embedded in building up your value system is the art of finding who you are, *'knowing yourself'*, this is the pursuit. This is the greatest purpose of man, the best gift to give oneself and the world. Without the primary self-values in life, it could prove exceedingly difficult to indulge oneself in creativity. There is a name for conformists in Nigeria- 'follow-follow', in other words following others blindly without your own 'WHY'. Remember your new endeavour is not common ground, your neighbour, family, or friends might not get it, you are pioneering something new, never been done before.

As a mother of three wonderful girls, I know what it means to birth someone. I appreciate my amazing husband for his great support during all three births, he was there by my side giving his very best, but guess what just like in that last moment before you hear the cry of a new life, NO ONE ELSE can do that last push, you're going to have to go it, Alone!

Something common to all pioneers is the value system to forge through, persevere to get the result. Tell yourself today, I'm not giving up till I deliver my product! Whether it's a service or a new way of thinking, a business, disruptive technology, a career or a completely new idea- you will face the same feelings of inadequacy and a desire to quit but - press on anyway, you'll be thankful you did in the end.

As an individual, I'm not good with fitting in with the crowd. Somewhere within, there has always been this pull towards having personal convictions and not flowing with something because it is good and acceptable by others. Don't get me wrong, I have friends, good ones too, however, my friends know it is not always easy to get me out,

I even constantly struggle to follow on with the trends. I would join in now and again but it would always be a challenge keeping up with such a lifestyle. Still on the topic of getting to know yourself, be comfortable with your differences, and stop trying to conform to others. Distinguish yourself!

What values do you hold?

What things would you never be caught doing?

What attitude do you have, and people know you for?

Without core values, it is impossible to sustain change, birth a new concept or even invent a new product. Achieving goals require persistence, will power- like an able colleague will say 'your will must be stronger than your skill', confidence - and may I iterate here that confidence is not the absence of FEAR, but the presence of WILL-POWER. A man without values will rob himself and others of great achievements and that kind of man can be dangerous.

4 Step Plan to building Self Values:

1. Putting your calling first.
2. Spend time thinking and listening without distraction (you will need to make the time for this, it will not just happen).
3. Follow your plans through even if you face obstacles (often you will find that what seemed to be an obstacle is waiting for you and hoping you will push through it). It's all part of the process so you can tell the story.
4. Write down wisdom you learn along the way.

5. Put them where you can see it and come back to it from time to time

So, the call to knowing yourself is an endless pursuit, you discover new things and your association and environment have a major influence on who you are becoming. One of the reasons Socrates is important is not because he became popular for any inventions, he was a revolutionist, many of his followers went on to achieve greater things than he did. But He dared to be different and stand out from the crowd. Following your call might just be the embryo of the birthing of the next BIG thing! Pursue it!

Discipline

Discipline is one value everyone has in different measures depending on how much one has trained oneself. For example, I mentioned earlier that I took time off and even fasted the day I found clarity. That is a discipline to my body, I had taught it.

In January 2016, for the first time, I trained my body to go without food or water for 10days. I had never done anything like this before that. I persevered by seeking wisdom on the subject matter and knew I would not die. The first three days were dire, I almost gave in but after that my body concurred, knowing I was not going to give in. A wise man once said, 'man shall not live by bread alone', and I had succeeded to teach my body this. My mind was clearer, I heard and knew what to do expressly. I regret not having learnt the habit of journaling at the time, as I would have been able to share more with you now.

Step by Step Action Plan to Optimise Time Usage on Personal Valued Habit

1. Identify one area of your self you want to Focus on e.g *I spend a lot of time on social media and get upset how disorganised some pages are. I have helped some friends revamp their pages.*
2. Designate time daily to improve that area e.g read a book on social media marketing from 7:00 – 7:30 am everyday.
3. Find an excellent professional in this field that I am happy to take their advice, now follow them.
4. Tell family and friends about your new habit to keep you accountable.

Chapter 2
The Battle

Epic movies are known for battles and those battles are known for battle cries. There are warriors on their horses chanting, fighting, mouthing a shout of fierce determination, not minding that they might die the next minute. However, that is not the best mindset for the battlefield. Instead of fighting with the mindset of probable defeat, I would rather fight with the mindset of definite victory where there is no backing down till the last foe is down and the banner of victory is lifted high and the head of the enemy's champ is down, and in my hand.

So was the dream in my sleep one night, only that the enemy had permeated right into me, he was not fighting from outside. He got way closer, into the closest parts, it makes me uneasy just sharing it. In the dream, I was fully aware of his presence but was unable to shed him off easily, like a leech attached to the skin.

As horrifying as this may be, I have researched leeches to discover that there is a method to severe this almost-monstrous creature from burrowing into your tissue. To do this, you will have to look for the oral sucker and place your fingernail on your skin directly next to it, slide your finger towards the oral sucker and push it away sideways, this will cause it to detach, simultaneously. Then pick or push at the larger end to cause the parasite to lose suction, and even though it may have reattached itself to the finger, you can easily flick it away.

I go through this analogy to say this, the battle of your destiny is fierce, a battle in your mind! It will take some conscious and methodological peeling away of unproductive and useless patterns of behaviour holding you back from achieving your dreams, and trust me, they will not let go easily. Take this from a person who had a dream for over ten years, incubating and believing every single year from 2006, that each new year will be the year. I had this dream on my new year's resolution list every year after 2006.

My true breakthrough came in 2018 when I started writing this book. I feel relieved from all that sucking from the leech. I have eventually mastered the method to peeling off the leech and I am now sharing it with you. As I type this, I have a smile on my face because finally, I have the right mindset for winning, perseverance, commitment and courage!

In my dream, I had to indulge this enemy, to make it think he had me, although I knew he didn't. However, I had to be careful not to get lost in the middle of my plan.

<u>Advantages of the Leech</u>

Leeches have benefits. In leech therapy, leeches are used to prevent tissue dying, by placing them on a finger or toe, underneath a flap of skin, it helps to remove clotted blood which reduces tension and improves blood flow in the small blood vessels and increasing blood circulation.

So when next you sigh because you are going through a tough situation and askWHY ME, remember that the situation is there to work on your weaknesses, to perfect your gifts and shape your values. That is what my tough situation did for me and is doing for me. Itis working on my weaknesses, perfecting my gifts and shaping my values to present me to the world a better version - new model, ungraded and polished to achieve more.

The commensurate action

People are like grass; their beauty is like a flower in the field

The grass withers and the flower fades
but the word of the Lord remains forever. 1 Peter 1:24

The corresponding act for your destiny must be inspired by someone greater than you, as you in yourself cannot know your way, Afterall, you can only see that which is right before you. When someone who sees all things begin to direct you on the way to turn, it will be inevitable for you to arrive at the desired or ultimate destination.

It is better to aim high and miss than to aim low and hit.

Les Brown

Like one of my favourite speakers Andrew Wommack says, 'most people aim for nothing and hit it every time'. Invoking a much higher help, divine assistance is key in fulfilling your life's destiny. The actions corresponding with the clarion call must be specific so that it should achieve the set goals.

If you are a Christian, you know that His thoughts for you are good and not evil to bring you to an expected end (Joel 29:11). So, this action ought to be purposeful, and everything, including people, is created for a purpose. The simplest way to seek the purpose of a thing is by finding it in the heart of the maker.

This mostly comes in the form of a manual ('Manu' - to make a factor, the factor that made it; 'aul' - thought). We read the manual to know the thoughts of the maker and the use of a thing, how much more people. I am a Christian and identify the Bible as the manual I go to understand God's mind when He created me and to know my usefulness.

> *When the purpose of a thing is not known, abuse is inevitable. unknown author*

More important is the fact that God said, 'Let us make man in our image.' God created man in His own image' (Genesis 1:26-27). So, without knowing what the manufacturer intended with his creation, abuse is inevitable. You cannot listen to other people's opinion and ignore the owner's manual, it cannot compare. It is God's creative power to think a thing and call it into existence. As a man thinks, so he is. So, you cannot be anything short of who you are in your mind. In other words, you are a product of your thoughts, so pay attention to those thoughts and do the deep work of self-analysis and realisation of self-worth. See yourself through the manufacturer's eyes so you can optimise your potential.

What do I consider to be a priority right now in my life? This is a pertinent question.

In this phase, I began to think I had wasted some years to indecisiveness or perhaps even to a lack of strong will to pursue or do what I believe I should do. I diligently pursued a course and threw myself wholly to it, but somewhere along the way, I faced some roadblocks and I stopped.

This posed imminent questions. Was I on the wrong course? Or simple as it is, was it not time? Perhaps I didn't read the manual right and was taking a wrong turn at the wrong time? All well said the important thing is I am still here and I will *keep moving*, I will have another go. We never really know except in hinds sight when we look back and it makes more sense overall. This is the spirit of a winner!

What is next?

I will continue daily to be grateful. I started a gratitude journal where I write at least one thing I am grateful for about my husband and my children. I will keep to this as it has changed my perspective on things. I have more clarity and even through the course of my day I see more things I am grateful for and focus on them as I stay positive and happy.

Where should I focus my energy?

At this time, I ought to give time to the things that are important to me, and I have found that during different phases of life, different things gain my focus.

Have you noticed when you focus on a problem, it becomes bigger than it seems and tends to become overwhelming and looks as though there is no way out? This is not true, If you go back to 'the battle' you remember I mentioned that 'the things that are seen are temporal, but the things that are not seen are eternal'. In other words, those thoughts in your mind are fighting for the chance to be actualised and even though you see a huge mountain right before you except you accept it as an insurmountable mountain and give up, that mountain couldn't be a real obstacle. You need to recondition your mind to know that there is a way out. There is a route to get to the other side and whether you find it or not will be very dependent on the values you have cultivated along the way. So, make sure you have mastered devoting time to that and focus your energy on divine solutions, insights and never on the problem.

There is nothing as powerful as an idea whose time has come.

Victor Hugo

All things are created twice: first in your mind, as a thought or dream, then in reality as a physical creation.

One Habit Daily that will Increase my Productivity

Monday   _____   _____

Tuesday   _____   _____

Wednesday _____   _____

Thursday   _____   _____

Friday   _____   _____

When you have a clear outcome you want to work on daily, then its just a matter of commitment and following it through weekly. 15 minutes daily quickly adds up to one hour thirty-five minutes a week working on a personal value. In no time this will become second nature, and you can replicate it.

Chapter 3
Know Your Mission Statement

By faith, we understand that the entire universe was formed at God's command, that what we now see did not come from anything that can be seen. Hebrews11:3

Beginning with the end in mind

Take charge of your mind and do not just allow it to wander around, follow world trends and dictates. This is a state of chaos, an unpleasant sight. Also where there is no direction nor purpose, abuse is inevitable. No wonder in Genesis1:1, *'the world was without form and void... and God said, let there be light, firmament, water, land, birds...man'*.Until you take charge of your mind and begin the creation in there, the physical creation can't happen.

Daniel Webster says

> *If we work upon marble, it will perish.*
> *If we work upon brass, time will efface it.*
> *But if we work upon immortal minds, and instil into them just principles,*
> > *we are then engraving upon tablets which no time will efface*

but will brighten and brighten to all eternity.

No wonder even God says the laws shall no longer be, this is the covenant I will make with them after that time, says the Lord. I will put my laws in their hearts, and I will write them on their minds (Hebrews 10:16)

The mind is an incredible place, capable of much more than we could ever imagine. It has a creative ability woven into it that allows it to wander and travel creating new things as the owner wishes. Can you practice going somewhere peaceful in your mind right now? You might have a lot on it but quieten it and narrow the thought back to a place of peace and tranquillity. A place where you were happy and bring it into your presence. Can you feel the smiles sipping through? Now, remember this next time you feel rotten. Also, remember that feelings and thoughts are temporal and very subjective to change, and guess who is in control of the change? YOU ARE!

Work on your mind, take control of it and tell it where you want it to go.

One day, about the time I started having these mind shifts and renewals, I had a heart to heart talk with my husband, I don't think I have ever felt like that, I perfectly understood his viewpoint. He is far advanced than I am in this mind game. He knows exactly how he feels and what He wants, it is a maturity I have always envied.

However that day, I realised I had lived with him for so long yet never allowed myself to be influenced by this kind of mindset. I can accept his superiority and mentorship and allow myself to change my deeply wired brain from being mostly in a soliloquy to being engaged with the world around me, and that's what I did. I worked on my mind.

The Wait

> *This vision is for a future time... if it seems slow in coming, wait patiently, for it will surely take place. It will not be delayed.*
>
> *Habbakuk2:2 -3*

The bible has ministered to me for years and is one of the things that infuse me with hope for the future. When we are hopeful, we radiate such glow and anticipation of something greater.

It is like when you are with your lover and you are expectant but then they surprise you on a bigger scale than your expectation, it brings tears to your cheeks not because you were not aware it would happen, but because how it happened was beautiful and it blew your mind. God is doing what is best for you and it will happen according to His schedule, not yours. Waiting can be daunting but wait in excitement for what is coming. Anticipate that something good is cooking and imagine yourself enjoying the outcome. This will help you wait well and in the end, it will be well worth the wait. Every seed disappears for a while before remerging on the outside, radiant, beautiful, and mightier. Wait for it!

The Distraction/ Opportunity Test

Many opportunities present themselves to an individual daily, some we take, others we ignore. Most times, because of who is offering an opportunity, we take the opportunity, not analysing its relevance to our individual goal or pursuit often leading to what I describe as the distraction. Remember I earlier described 'the battle'. It is real, whether you accept it or not, some powers contend with you for your core call.

Would you rather you follow someone else's lane, lose time in the pursuit of your call and deviate into someone else's lane, a lane where you could never reap a finisher's reward, where you could be disqualified? Or run yours well, may be slow or you get to your destination and receive a great reward.

When opportunities come, it is time to analyse its relevance to you. I have often heard when you get an opportunity, opt-in, and learn later. This does not sound right. It goes against God's principle that 'the steps of the righteous are ordered by God'. There is a path to step into, not all roads lead to success, or shall I say, 'good success'. There is a success that befits you and even though I do not have all the answers, I trust that if you stay with me till the end we will soon discover the way to achieve it.

Now, when opportunities come your way before you grab it with both hands, you will do yourself a lot of good if you ask yourself the following questions.

1. What are my goals?
2. How much time will I need to put in?
3. Do I have this extra time without it affecting my focus or goal?

If you answer these questions honestly, you will know whether the opportunity before you is a worthy one or a distraction, something to take you away from your original focus.

The biggest obstacles I have had to overcome are these self-doubts, and Loss of a loved one. While those incidences were hard on me, I can't deny that they taught me some great lessons in life and they are part of my strong foundation.

What I learnt and how it is helping me today

I learnt that I need to be grateful for the life that I have. No one owes me, especially not God. Whether I am here or not, God remains God, so I never blame him for what goes wrong in my life. Rather I thank him for the good things He does for me and praise Him that I know He is bigger than the negatives. This is a process that has so many facets or levels. You finish one and walk into the next 'class of life'. Maybe time management module, positive thinking module, personal development module, listening to yourself and taking your own-advice-first module and many more.

The downtimes and uptimes of my life have made me a great worshipper. It enlightened me to see from a different perspective, a viewpoint I had not focussed on before. Knowing I am the architect of my future and that whilst I have life, I need to make the most of it. Doing the things I love and learning each day regardless of whether I make a mistake in those things or not.

I have been journaling long before the hype it now receives. Keeping a diary, writing down my thoughts, people sometimes even think I am writing too much, but I do not believe there is any such thing. I believe your notes are to your future self. Inevitably you would not remember all the thoughts and feelings you have in life, some that are important to who you become will get documented on those pages. Oftentimes reading through my journal inspires me today. 'I can't believe I wrote that' often runs through my mind. There are great lessons you can learn from yourself. The school of life teaches you all there is to learn, but are you paying attention to the lessons? Do you even know what class you are in now or the next one you are heading into? Pay attention to the lessons because it will greatly determine how far you go and how quickly you get there.

Excellence

Be excellent! Stop comparing yourself with others. There is a difference between imitation and Inspiration. Dare to live your dream. Let the world see you vulnerable. You might need to go down first before you go up. You are the one in that process- work it through, without quitting at any stage of it. When you continue to compare yourself, you sell yourself short. When you compare with someone lower, you OVERESTIMATE yourself and when you compare with someone higher you OVERWHELM yourself. So, let's not go over, let us just stay in lane and maintain a steady growth upwards, you being the judge whilst the environment around you remains the yardstick.

Zig Ziglar puts it this way:

> *Success means doing the best we can with what we have. Success is the doing, not the getting, not the triumph. Success is a personal standard, reaching for the highest that is in us, becoming all that we can be.*

While you are seeking excellence- you would be surprised at the result and your capabilities that you can never discover in someone else and by imitating them.

It is becoming increasingly difficult to be authentic in this age. Considering the level of exposure that social media affords. My greatest worry is for the young millennials, who do not know otherwise, have never lived a life where they were not so involved in someone else's private life with the pressures it brings. With no true perspective that people don't share their worst moments, but only pictures of their perfect meal, achievements, leaving a bitter taste of 'I'm never doing enough' and not considering how much editing and filtering has gone into the picture or video.

The mind is a powerful place but constantly feeding it with negativity will not equip it to offer you its best results. So, see and think less of negativity, dream, aspire and achieve more.

This pushed me to seek answers, what exactly is God's will for me? How do I make the most of my own time and birth a new vision and purpose in life?

Once you've discovered it, share it and make it inspirational.

Sharing your story is a beautiful thing. Everyone likes stories. That is why we scroll through profiles, get hooked on motivators who tell good ones, and keep seeking meaningful ones we can relate with, stories sustain us and are nice to hear or watch.

We get drawn to stories that inspire us and reveal the innate ambition that propels a copycat. Watch the stories that you are drawn to, that is the area of your purpose, impacting performance and ability to go on and become.

Stories are inspiring. Yours, if written and shared will go on to inspire others. Ever heard the saying 'there is nothing new under the heavens?' It is very true when I read stories of heroes that have lived, fictional or not. I see the same trend happening over and over where good overcomes evil, even sometimes when it looks like it takes a very long time to achieve, in the end, it always happens. Or when a man is captured and out of his captivity, he summons some strength, tenacity, and resilience, and finds a way out to become an extraordinary being and saves the day.

That is how ordinary people become a lifetime hero, by weathering on, striving and never giving up until they find their win and tell their stories.

I hope I am inspiring you to decide to live your story so you or another might tell it.

How to get a promotion

To qualify for a promotion or a progression, you should have completed the present phase and every agenda on that stage or subject as required. And everyone is at this stage in one way or the other. It might be financial, career, education, goals, family, emotions and so on. Regardless of what area this might be, I want you to forget every societal prejudice and understand that promotion ultimately comes from God. Psalm 75: 6-7

'So, are you saying it does not matter the tone of my skin, the level of my education, the prejudice in my workplace, the fact that my boss doesn't like me and ...?' Yes, I mean just that. Regardless of all these things, promotion comes from God.

I came to an understanding of this and it brought about a shift in my mindset and priorities in life. Therefore, what are the criteria for promotion and advancement if they are not these things I just mentioned above? This brings me to the topic in more depth.

We will look at this criterion based on the story of Daniel. A guy whom the bible records as a man with an excellent spirit. He was considered eligible for the promotion. He came highly recommended by the queen mother in his old age as someone who would have the answer when all the scholars and knowledgeable professors in the land had no answer for the king.

He was first encountered by the king when he alongside his three other friends was captured and decided to set themselves apart by choosing their diet carefully, making a choice not to be gluttonous when at the king's banquet.

The Character

They did the work with all their heart even when no one was looking, their attitude of being conscientious was noticeable.

No wonder the phrase 'action speaks louder than words' because it reflects the true nature of your heart. If you want to get a promotion at work and want your boss to promote you, quit 'eye-service'. Regardless of how you think this gets you noticed, people can tell 'genuine people' and when it gets to the crux of the matter, that always supersedes.

Attitude and Character

Excellence is an attitude, an intentional attitude that can never be achieved haphazardly. It is impossible to achieve your best without preparation and intentionality because like one of my favourite speakers always says 'the stream always flows to the lowest parts by default, it will require a great effort to flow upward' that's because everything in life achieved is by default, except consciously programmed to function otherwise.

Excellent means to be

> *'particularly good of its kind, eminently good, first-class or superior'*
> *'Greatness- the absolute best. It is the quality of excelling, of being truly the best at something'*

Having talked about the spirit of excellence, a lot of us think it is impossible and have also chosen to have an impossible mindset about certain situations.

There are three other attributes I would like to add to this, which are awe, gratitude, and altruism.

An emotional feeling of awe and connection to something bigger increases your self-value and perception, making you aware of a bigger picture than yourself and giving you something to work towards. Awe by itself would not give purpose but coupled with gratitude and altruism, it is dynamic for an explosive impact in your immediate environment and potentially even a larger following.

As a teenager, one of the phrases that inspired me was 'crowd puller'. It all happened one day when the Holy Spirit dropped it in my heart, I have been living up to it ever since and that is what a sense of purpose is - when you have an end in mind, one so much bigger than you that in your present state it seems impossible to attain by yourself.

However, with the right attitude and character fostered in you, it becomes possible.

It becomes possible when you never give up as you constantly live every moment in anticipation of the future moment where you would reach that desired end. This is hope!

Do not mistake this hope for the absence of fear or doubt at times. It is human to forget a thing, but the importance of writing it down cannot be overemphasized. Because those notes, in your younger self's handwriting or typed note on google docs (we are in a new era... laughing) will remind you of who you are when life tries to knock you down and tell you to give up on yourself.

Five Questions to Ask Family and Friends To Identify Your uniqueness

1. What do you think I am good at?
2. What mark do you think I will leave on the world?
3. When do you think I am most engaged?
4. What do you think are my greatest strengths?
5. What gets my attention all the time?

Look beyond your immediate horizon to the far future. What do you see yourself doing? Your dreams are not born when they are actualised. They have been a part of you right from the beginning, but the spotlight turns on them at different times by the situation at hand. So, spending some time to do some soul searching and thinking is good practice. Reach within and fish out your purpose and what you were made for. I understand your environment does play a part in what you do and the debate on nature/nurture is not one I intend to begin now, but if you are honest and factual enough you would see the prints on the wall and the little writings all along trying to stir you in the right direction.

God's plan is what unfolds regardless of your many desires.

Your Personal Mission Statement

_____
_____
_____
_____
_____
_____
_____

Now that you have identified what you want to spend your time on, Plan how you will do it in short bursts of time.

Chapter 4
Identity

Know yourself but more importantly, be disciplined!

Kendal Bronk, a leading expert on purpose wrote, 'the rare condition of leading a life of purpose is associated to physical wellbeing - good sleep, less chronic pain, and longevity of life'.

psychological health = happiness, hope and satisfaction in life

Know who you are!

When you know who you are and what you stand for or represent, you are one step closer to achieving your purpose per time. We have been looking at Daniel's life and how he knew his God. That confidence in God and the loyalty he had to God made him stand for his God even when he wasn't sure his God would come through for him. This kind of knowing and loyalty only comes as a result of intentionality and consciousness of who you are.

Like a prince would carry himself with class regardless of who is watching. A prince who knows and has accepted who he is doesn't wait to be monitored or cajoled into carrying out his princely duties and lifestyle. He is always conscious of carrying himself like a king. Your life is beyond you and understanding that there is a power or purpose bigger than yourself is one step towards achieving the kind of excellence that goes beyond a superficial level. There is a bigger driving force, and more is going to be required of you to achieve this.

Be passionate

What you are passionate about can come on a spectrum of innate social constructs. Oftentimes, I have this discussion on nature vs nurture where I discuss with various people asking them to tell me which they find more influencing. Even though I believe more in nurture, I have concluded that both play a vital role in who you as an individual. Also, what you are passionate about tells the kind of individual that you are. Your passions are a mixture of having studied your history and identified what they are known for and the deep passions that resonate with you as an individual which you naturally gravitate towards.

Hard work

Excellence can be achieved but not without some hard work. It doesn't fall on laps, it is worked at. It is not also restricted to some set of rules and some 'dos and don'ts'. To achieve excellence, you need perseverance, self-control, determination, and a clear goal/vision insight. Practising excellence is staying committed to your goals and vision even when you do not feel like it.

Activation energy

This is required to get your ass out of a warm bed and into a cold outdoor, excuse my language. You must take the job to parent yourself, to tell yourself to do the things you need to do but do not feel like doing. That's how you were parented and if you are a parent, that is how you parent your kids and yourself too. Lead yourself first before you get to lead others.

You are never going to feel like doing it, so Just do it! It is simple to change not easy!

It's interesting to note that there are *two sides of the brain. There is the* autopilot. Here, a person functions at a low level and the emergency brake is always active. Usually, any time there is a break from routine, the brakes surface, the brain functions in auto-pilot to keep you stuck in the mire of routine.

Routine can be draining.

Whenever you feel stuck, dissatisfied, bored, it is most likely that your soul needs exploration and growth, which can only happen by forcing yourself out of your head!

Forcing yourself to be uncomfortable! Challenges cure boredom!

get OUT of your head

get PAST your feelings

get OUTSIDE your comfort zone

Feelings are to be ignored especially when it comes to productivity. Following your feelings can hinder the speed you need to accomplish. When you do not take risks but stay in your comfort zone always, your success can be hindered. Get outside, that is where the action is!

The 5-second rule

This is the concept of acting on thoughts on or before five seconds from the time it was conceived. You face it and act in 5 seconds else the emergency brake will be pulled, and you will KILL the idea and then it won't be anyone's fault but yours. Always practice the 5 seconds rule. Practice the 5-second rule on impulse. Experiment with it.

Words

The 'WORD' is the creator. Do you know that research by neurosurgeons suggests that the part of the brain that controls speech is in charge of the nerves all over your body? So your speech, the words you speak are the most important in this journey of creating or inventing that imagination in your heart. The lingering thought that will not let you be, it keeps you up at night, you share with the wrong people and you stand the chance of being labelled 'crazy'. I know you know what I am talking about because you have had that imagination since you were a kid, and you are on the verge of giving up on it.

PAUSE! Just before you do, can I invite you to try one last time?

During the 2020 Corona Virus pandemic, a historic time in my lifetime, a season like no other one I have ever experienced, I got an epiphany. The period was so scary and overwhelming that many said it was like a war - a pandemic that had taken the world by storm - the Coronavirus.

As I write this, it is still present and affecting lives. When it was on the rise, it infected people so rapidly that governments had to shut down the economy. Children were home, parents who could were working from home, no one on the streets, shops closed. It was like a compulsory holiday only that Mums and Dads were the chefs, teachers, friends, entertainers and so on.

In the middle of the pandemic, I found time to critically take a look at the potency of words.

I was studying along the lines of communication and I discovered that to influence people you ought to be deliberate about it. To influence yourself, you need to use the right vocabulary. This was the epiphany. **I WANT TO BE UNAPOLOGETIC ABOUT HOW I USED WORDS AS REGARDS MY LIFE. IT'S MY LIFE AND I HAVE TO BE DELIBERATE ABOUT THE WORDS I USE ABOUT MY LIFE.**

Instead of thinking about the negatives, fear, and impossibilities, that the pandemic was casting upon me, I began using positive words.

Do you know that using words like 'I am sufficient', can create the world you want to achieve? Those words are potent enough to create a world where the manifestation of those words will be a reality. Remember your words can create for you the thoughts and imaginations of your heart. The earlier you get this, the quicker you can see your dreams become realities

The words we speak are the creator of our world. Those that know the power of their words will see supernatural occurrences.

In a study by the Human Engineering Lab, they tracked thousands of successful people from all fields, industries, and disciplines. The goal was to uncover the traits that successful people share. There was only one common trait that was consistent with all the participants, they all have a large vocabulary. The president of Harvard's Human Engineering Lab, Johnson O'Connor, addressed the question, why do large vocabularies characterize executives and outstanding men and women?

"The final answer," O'Connor said, "seems to be that words are the instruments, by means of which, men and women grasp the thoughts of others and which they do much of their own thinking. They are the tools of thought."

'Words are the tools of thought'. Neuroscientists have recently discovered about the brain, and how the brain uses words to think and, in turn, solve problems, innovate and create. There were other researches done by this institute relating to rank on the corporate ladder, becoming an executive, status, and income potential. To see more check out the studies by the institute.

The Good Book puts it this way 'the power of life and death lies in the tongue'. It is a little member that controls the whole body. It is not too late to begin to work on that language, vocabulary, and its use.

These are a few words that are positive and empowering and I would love you to explore these words.

CONSISTENCY: a harmonious uniformity or agreement among things or parts

CREATIVITY: the ability to bring something into existence

DEDICATION: complete and wholehearted fidelity

EFFORT: use of physical or mental energy; hard work

EMPOWERMENT: the act of conferring legality or sanction or formal warrant

INVESTING: the act of investing

LEARNING: the cognitive process of acquiring skill or knowledge

OPEN-MINDED: ready to entertain new ideas

OPPORTUNITY: a possibility from a favourable combination of circumstances

PERSEVERANCE: the act of persisting

PROSPEROUS: in fortunate circumstances financially

SACRIFICE: the act of forgoing your natural tendency for a cause

TEACHING: the activities of educating or instructing

VISION: the ability to see

RESILIENCY: the ability of a material to return to its original shape

ATTITUDE: a complex mental state involving beliefs and feelings

ALTITUDE: Elevation above sea level or the earth's surface

CHARACTER: A property that defines the individual nature of something

ENDURANCE: A state of surviving; remaining alive

ACTIVITY

Which of the words above will you use when describing yourself?

Now, regarding your call and vision, write down your vocabulary on it. What is your character towards it? Write it down too!

What words do you use to describe your achievement?

What do you say about yourself achieving your dreams in the subject area? With the words you have written down, go to work, speaking. Get speaking and creating the world you want to see with the words that represent the future you want to see rather than speaking words to describe what you see at the moment.

Let us look at Genesis 1 for a minute. A case study of God creating the world.

The History of Creation

1 In the beginning God created the heavens and the earth. 2 The earth was without form, and void; and darkness [a]was on the face of the deep. And the Spirit of God was hovering over the face of the waters.

3 Then God said, "Let there be light"; and there was light. 4 And God saw the light, that it was good; and God divided the light from the darkness. 5 God called the light Day, and the darkness He called Night.]So the evening and the morning were the first day.

6 Then God said, "Let there be a firmament in the midst of the waters, and let it divide the waters from the waters."

So here we see God looking at a dark space with nothing in it, but what I see here is someone who had envisioned something he could not see yet but spoke what was in His imagination. His first statement 'let there be light' was Him speaking directly to the darkness. He was not saying 'there will be light in the future', neither did he say 'there is no darkness', which will be a denial of the obvious. But rather He spoke the positive. What he saw was darkness. But he never used darkness in His statement, He spoke light (positive) expression, that is opposite of what was right before his eyes. Can you practice that with your current situation? Have a go and say what will be the positive speech to create the imagination of your heart concerning that situation.

The next statement from him was that He saw that it was good. The minute He saw what He imagined before his face, he was inspired to say something else.

When you begin speaking or creating your world, it becomes easier to create more like it. Once, you grasp this little activity, you are on your way to creating a world you have always dreamt of but never had the nerves to create.

Start with your words!

Self Affirmations

I am sufficient

I have what it takes

I am a solution bearer

People are waiting for me to find my voice so I can help them

Some people need me to change their lives

I take my position now and step up to bring a solution to my world

Talk to yourself, the same way you would talk to those people you are sent to. The first step of mastery is to have solved your problem yourself, so you can be confident enough to know you can solve for others.

I once had a pyjama that read, 'sleep less, dream more!' Yes, that's true! Who has sleep helped? I say this in my Nigerian accent, laughing. The more you dream it, the more you speak it and the more real it is to you and in no time, you will see it.

<u>Speak</u>

Words are the creator of your world, the changer of your present circumstance and the revealer of the future you hope for. In other to be able to see something different from what you are experiencing now, there must be a shift in the words you speak. Where you are now is a result of the world you have created before now, whether you consciously created this world is another thing.

Today, I urge you to be more conscious of the future you now hope to have. Not in wishful thinking, but out of a confident expectation, speak to the world what you want to see. Use your words to paint the picture of your future.

'I have what my clients need. I provide solutions to their problems by reducing their stress and increasing their pleasures. I bring joy to the world and the world is a better place because of me. People seek me to speak about my expertise because I add value to them, and they are willing to pay for it. I am a bestselling author and my books bring in millions. People are blessed when they read my books and know what to do with their time. They have clarity in their mind and find their purpose in life.'

Here is a proclamation of my future, the one I wish to see as regards my book.

So, life is deliberate, and it is all contained in the words you speak today. Speak to the situation, it has ears, laughing. It is funny but it is true because the situation speaks to you all the time. Not in audible voices, you can hear, but in the influence, it has on your mind. Have you seen how the bill that comes through your letterbox, sends shivers down your spine when you open it? You have to speak back at it, say it out loud, 'I will pay this bill in time'. That will send a message to your mind which will, in turn, put you into action to work out what you have spoken about your near future.

Accompanying the words you speak closely, is the mindset you have.

Mindset shift

The mind is the home of imaginations. Have you heard the popular saying 'as a man thinks, so is he'? It is a word inspired by the wisest of all. The thoughts of a man's heart are numerous. We think between 60000 to 80000 thoughts in one day, that is about 2500 to 3300 thoughts per hour. That is incredible, isn't it?

But are you conscious of those thoughts? And productive in its use? If you paid attention to them, you would realise that most of them are *useless* unimportant thoughts and they pass through the mind at a huge speed. They are words you repeat in your mind to yourself- let's say they are conversations you have with yourself, things you've heard said, questions- some of which you did not even seek or pursue the answers to, answers- that you did not bother to act upon, and a lot of senseless wandering thoughts. Like a huge train terminal or airport, where a lot of people come and go with no one living there.

To be more conscious of these numerous thoughts, try to study, plan, or solve a problem. Suddenly, you would realise the many straying thoughts clamouring for your attention, like a butterfly flying from flower to flower not staying still on one.

Now that we have ascertained that the thoughts run wild and keep running, as the engine of your vehicle running even when you are not going anywhere as it is parked in the driveway, that is how your thoughts are an automatic process that cannot be stopped. It can be tiring or exhausting at times, that is why some resort to drugs, drinking, or to developing hobbies and drown themselves in numerous activities to keep their minds engaged. But is that really what you should be doing? Is there a better way to harness our mind and put our thoughts to better use in other to achieve the results of a better future? Is there any way to put the energy and time to better use, have a better focus and increase productivity? Or is it just inner peace and calm that is not drenched in drinks and drugs with no true awareness or enjoyment of the peace you so desperately seek?

What you have in your future is so much bigger that if you can see it, you would not be disappointed over the little loss in the present. Keep keeping on and you will see that future lives out right before your eyes. When you are finally there you will not complain about your past!

So, do not just think you will do it, or plan to do it, do it.

Meditation

I'm sure you would have heard this word used quite often recently, but in my opinion, meditation is a conscious action to think on a specific topic per time. A heightened awareness of your thought and steering them in the direction you want it to go. You may ask, so how do I do that? In my experience, this is best done in the morning, when your mind has received rest from the thousands of thoughts that have been running wild from the previous day, so right from the start of the day take a hold on it. Do not allow it to run wild and control you. Speak words like

I have control of my mind

I have clarity and I am focused

I know what to do and I make decisive choices today

And if you are a believer of Jesus say

Holy spirit I listen to your whispers today

I have solutions and inspirations that I will follow to achieve my expected end

Again, during the day, pick a time, a signal, attach it to an ongoing habit, or perhaps lunchtime. This will be a reminder to meditate again. It is a conscious exertion of inner strength or energy which I believe you will be willing to do. Consider it an exercise to strengthen the muscles of your mind. By the time you master it or have exercised it enough, it will be second nature, with no more pain but more gains. There are benefits of a strengthened, focus mind that can achieve all that it is set to do. The benefits outweigh the work required.

This effect of meditation is so important because it will influence the words that come out of your mouth. Have you met people who lash out when driving? Who use swear words and are uncontrollable in their anger? Take a look at their life, they have not mastered harnessing their mind. They are not in control of their thoughts, so the words flow out of their mouth uncontrollably and inevitably wrong words also.

Read

Before you meditate, there is something more important. Reading! Yes, reading the Bible and saying the scriptures. I already emphasised on meditation, the words you speak out. It is a cycle. The words you speak out are influenced by what you have read and heard which in turn influences your actions and then the level of your success.

You need to know what to say, so this step is especially important. Otherwise, anything could come out of your mouth. So, reading cannot be omitted. When you only allow the right words out of your mouth just after a major win, imagine a fortress guarded by soldiers. In today's terms, a gold bank guard does the job of guarding the gold bank with his life. He remains alert and watches who goes in and out. How much more the mind, you ought to guard it, so that only the right words get out of your mouth. That is why we will only allow into our mind, through reading, the right content. Stories of heroes in your field, people who have been what you now want to become. This can also be in the form of attending college or university to study a subject area where you intend to be known for.

Act

Have ever thought about your actions? What exactly is your motive for the action you are taking? Take for example your decision and preparation for a presentation to your boss or course tutor, you want him to get the gist of your paper, you also want him/ her to see you as confident, knowledgeable and organised.

So, you put an effort into your presentation slide, making it beautiful and saying the right words and using the right body language included. Can you see how interwoven the thoughts, words, action, and success(results) are? And then it starts again. We need to master each of this step to achieve the result we intend each time.

There are so many excuses we can make when we do not want to do something, even when we know it is the right thing to do. Seeking validation from someone else, just to reaffirm our fears and when we do not get the response we desire, we look somewhere else hoping to eventually find someone who will stand by your desire. Just stop losing to yourself and follow through what you know you have got to do.

Are you radical enough to seek out how to help others?

Do you just forgive or wait for others to come forward first?

Are you self-disciplined?

Are you patient?

Do you love others and wish to serve or care for them?

It's easy to read this book that I've spent more than 500 hours writing, or even nod your head in agreement, perhaps underline some words in it but the real challenge is *acting* on what you have read and taking the time to make it matter now that you have reaffirmed to yourself that these things are important to your purpose in life. So, what we think we know does not matter, what matters is what we do with our time.

I am not in any way saying any of these tasks are easy. I am just saying with the right tools and right mindset, we can change the words we speak, begin to see the imaginations of our hearts and succeed in this lifetime. This is called painting a new future for yourself.

Courage

Courage is not the absence of fear. It is an ability to do something that frightens you and have strength through it even in the face of pain or grief, with an assurance of a positive outcome. Courage is somewhat greater than being brave, it is the traits, motivations and thoughts that go through a man when faced with a decision or action.

Can I burst the myth that certain people are brave, and others are not? Courage can be learnt and when you begin to tip and dive into it, you find out, it's scarier on the outside than on the inside.

On the outside, you do not know what to expect, so this generates a fear of its own, another thing that happens on the outside is the powerlessness to influence anything or change anything. You are just there wishing and hoping without action. Whereas on the inside, you can impose, you can suggest and influence the course of action and history forever. Courage opts you in! It is the secret ingredient the achievers have over non-achievers, doers overs hearers, and successful over 'wannabes'.

There is physical, emotional, social, moral, intellectual, and spiritual courage. Physical courage popularly termed 'bravery' is the most conspicuous. It's exhibited in the face of the risk of bodily harm or death. Developing your resilience, physical strength or awareness can increase a person's physical courage.

Another one that is becoming more prevalent in our age is social courage, involving the risk of a social embarrassment, exclusion or rejection and unpopularity. People with social courage rise as leaders in their community.

Intellectual courage is exhibited when you are willing to challenge the status quo, engage with your ideas and risk making mistakes that might as well be revolutions.

A lot of people lack this, but the few that master this courage, live with fewer regrets. It is an ability to do the right thing with the risk of disapproval, shame, and opposition from others. Not about who we say we are but rather through integrity and ethics revealed in your actions to others.

Emotional Courage is an openness to the full spectrum of positivity risking encountering the negative thoughts. In other words, you act on your emotions despite your fear of the outcome.

And lastly, Spiritual Courage, intricately linked to purpose, meaning, and faith. A strong belief in a course and innate strength to pursue.

That last one can be fuelled by knowledge. Knowledge of the backing of someone greater than you are. So, the bigger your backing, and the knowledge of them, the more courageous you are. Like when a soldier goes to war, they know they have the supplies and backing of their sponsor. American soldiers, for example, go knowing they have supplies, they have confidence in the person who has sent them, so they match in boldly ready to take the territory they are entering and conquer.

How is courage developed? You have been exhibiting courage for a long time. When you took your first steps as a baby, and your Mum was so ecstatic as you carried on, that was courage. When you learnt to ride a bike, that was courage. Now, those sseemingly simple acts have become second nature. When you stood up to the class bully and he never picked on you again, when you started your business online, when you wrote your book, when you welcomed a stranger and conversed and now you're married, all these are expressions of courage.

Courage is putting your fears aside and taking the first steps, will it be scary? Yes, but do it anyway. Will it be worth it? Absolutely YES, even if it does not achieve the outcome expected, you are strengthening that courage muscles whether it's physical, social, emotional, or spiritual.

Courage is an action, a decisive one, acting where a risk is involved. Courage is essential to achieve growth.

Courage will help you

1. Build confidence and self-trust.
2. Set achievable goals and relish the achievement.

3. Manage fear by focusing on the course at hand and never on the feeling and thoughts of fear.
4. Create opportunities to practice and persevere through activities and hobbies that you enjoy by setting goals to achieve the next stage. Constantly learn new skills.
5. Be part of a community that promotes a sense of belonging and self-worth. Be a contributor to the course and get feedback on your work or appraisal of your achievements.

This list is inexhaustible, and you should constantly grow. Your choice to read this book is a step in the right direction and a time well spent, especially if you follow it with commensurate actions and targets.

Resolute

Being comfortable about being uncomfortable is a place to aspire to be and reach because until then, you can't achieve a purpose. One of the things I reflect on when it is my birthday is, 'how comfortable am I being uncomfortable now?' And as the years went by, I have become less concerned about what people think and more determined to reveal my awesomeness to my world. You have awesomeness to reveal and it is so unfair when you choose to be selfish with it.

Life is for giving not gathering. There is this paradox of life that the one that scatters gathers more. If you think you are not growing, start giving. Invest in someone else, help them grow and make them better, you would be surprised how much this will help you grow yourself.

A particularly good example is a parent, one that is reflective. I know when I correct my child, I must grow in that area too because mummy cannot be seen living short of her advice. Teaching others raises your bar of attainment. It forces you to grow!

'Whether I perish I perish', No longer fearful of failure. Failure is an evil tyrant! One that should be dealt with and put in its place. Facing life with an attitude of not fearing failure opens an opportunity to succeed.

When you are no longer scared of dying, you live

When you do not fear failure, you succeed

When you do not fear war, you pursue peace

When you do not fear rejection, you make a friend

When you do not fear the waves you surf

When you do not fear the height, you jump

And only then do you become a record-breaker.

The fear of failure demoralises you. But when you use your fear, you are strengthened and stand a better chance at success. Fear is one of your tools for success. It drives you to do your research. It helps you weigh your risks before making your decision. However, it should never stop you from acting.

When you get to the other side, only then do you realise that there was nothing there stopping you but yourself. You might say to me, 'but I have failed a few times in the past', and I say 'ok, but you have learnt one or maybe even ten more ways not to do it'. So, here is what am saying; failure is part of success! You can't avoid it, so do not let failure stop you, rather ride on failure and get to your destination, Succeed!

Your will is more powerful than you think. Especially if you believe.

Every year people make a 'new year's resolution', I don't know whether to call this a scam or not, but I know it never really worked for me. It sounds like something like this

'This year I will write my book.'

'This year I will quit smoking.'

'This year I will be a better friend.'

An ambiguous resolution leaves you clueless, you end up not even knowing how to achieve it. So, the resolution here must target your character and put in place actions to counter them to get the different result you aspire for. So instead put it like this- SMART (Specific, Measurable, Attainable, Relevant, Timebound) and place it in a place you can see it.

'My book is going to help people make better use of their time and will empower them to live a life of purpose.'

'I will write 2 pages a day.'

'I will be happier when I reach people, I can't get the chance to speak awesomely and personally to people through my book.'

'By November of this year, I will launch my book.'

So, get writing and be resolute on your outcome. Result, Purpose, and Massive Action (RPM) will guide you in your writing later in this book. You will be an achiever by the time you finish this.

This is how I wrote down my goals to complete this book you are reading and here it is now, in your hands, blessing you. This is how you must set your own goals.

SLEEP

I did not think I would add this to this, but eh! Here it is. Sleep is essential and I do not think anyone can stress that enough to you. At this junction, one thing I want to stress is the need to know yourself. A lot of motivators have written about rising early and getting out of bed early but tiredness, lethargy, can be signs of other mental health issues or medication.

So, getting good quality sleep can result in better results, concentration, and that success you so desperately are trying to attain by avoiding sleep in the first place.

According to research, up to one-third of the population can be affected by insomnia (lack of sleep) and the ripple effect of this on our productivity, relationships, and ability to function through the day can be devastating. You should find basic techniques that can improve your quality of sleep or speak to your doctor about it.

I try not to judge myself. I like to sleep and sometimes I find that I need my sleep during the day and I take it. Yes, I said it! I take naps during the day at times because without it I am not productive anyway so why stay awake just to prove to people that I stay awake through the day. And sometimes I sleep for 8-10 hours at night. Don't misunderstand me, life is demanding and some of us cannot afford to sleep as long as we want, but know this one thing, when you know the importance of the tasks you perform in life, you do them unapologetically because the results speak for themself hence you work hard to make them affordable for you.

There was a particular day, I woke up at 5 am, Ok before you praise me, hear this. I went to bed without making dinner, now is another time to thank God for a loving husband.

He sorted the kids and did not wake me up. When I woke up, I was refreshed, did my devotion, prayed and with a new perspective I wrote this book for four hours nonstop and it flowed easily. This can only be attributed to good sleep!

WORK

Work cannot be substituted for any of the steps above. I'm sure you were not hoping that was the case, if you were, then pardon me if I call you lazy! (Raising my eyebrows with a little smirk on my face.)

Work will be required, my friend. Work is what brings results. So, when used with all that we have spoken about already. BOOM! A great reward for success is recorded.

So, what is work?

To define work here, I am not necessarily talking about a means of earning an income or 'the place where one is employed' but more about 'the task or tasks to be undertaken',

'a thing or things done or made: the result of an action'.

The ability to exercise the power of your will to take authority over things believing all that has been said to see an expected result is called faith. This faith is determined by your tenacity to do the work required with the hope that the outcome will be positive and not give up even when it doesn't seem like you are forging through. This faith is being certain and believing that the outcome is possible and it is the only result you choose to accept.

That's it. You need to act on your beliefs.

You might ask, how do I know what action to take that will be commensurate to the belief that I am an author? It is simple- WRITE. In a book, on a computer, on the web, on a blog, just write, begin writing and see where your heart leads you coupled with everything else, we have already talked about in this book.

For example, as an author myself, the words I speak to myself daily is this:

I will do well as an author

I will be wealthy selling my books and easily

I will be sought to speak because I master my subject

I am a blessing to my generation

I have the word of wisdom and knowledge

I know what to do and as I do it lines are falling to me in pleasant places

My eBook will become an extra stream of income to pay me millions

I did not just sit back and speak these words to myself, but because I believe them with all my heart, I began to write and the more I wrote, the lengthier the pages began to roll. And voila, here you are- one of the blessed people whom I spoke about that will buy my book and be blessed by it. Never mind even if you did not pay for it. You are still reading it and am sure you will buy some of my other books as the times go by.

So, the ball is in your court now! The choice is entirely yours, whether you will be a person who just has faith but goes to his/ her grave believing and never acting on it or that person who will read this and 'work' their ass off, acting upon their beliefs because you refuse to see your dreams remain dreams rather you choose to see them actualised and lived out.in your lifetime.

When I started doing the work, some things had to give. There were days I was so buried in my work, I hardly got up to eat. I felt like I had to keep going, if only I keep working at this pace, I will get the work done in no time. but then, I remembered I could burn out and that was no good for me or for the wonderful kids I have. I could break down and end up losing more work time and cause a delay in completing the work and I am drilling myself to accomplish. So, striking a balance in work is essential. I work hard following my very 'flexible routine 'and do the best I can.

The word 'flexible routine' came from my experience in managing nurseries. I did this for over 10 years of my life. What is that? It is a routine to be followed right, but the flexibility element makes it human. I spoke later in this book about 'will' and about 'time', where I share my example of a routine. The flexibility means allowing myself to let the routine give my day some sort of guidance, to allow accomplishing balanced and varied activities, making sure every element of my goal in life and for the season finds its place in my daily activities. The summation of those activities over time is my reality for the future. So next time you want to peek into the future, take a stock of your daily activities today, you will get a mirage of what lies ahead.

Chapter 5
Realization

Time

My last subject is *'Time'* because time never goes on forever. No matter how young you are reading this book, time passes by so quickly.

I remember in my late 30's speaking to a friend on a video chat once. It was her birthday and she joked, laughingly about how long we had known each other, from our teenage years, and now, wives, and mums to wonderful children. We reminisced over the good life we have had and how blessed we were but also how time had gone so quickly. I remember her even saying sarcastically, 'I am still 25...' in her Nigerian accent. Time does indeed go so quickly and the only comfort we derive from it is seizing each moment and making the most of the time we have because tomorrow is not guaranteed to anyone.

I heard this saying once *'Time is all we are given to exchange for everything else we have'*, It is so true. Time is what you exchange for money, friendship, rest, wisdom, knowledge, love, food and so on. You can put anything else you have and value in that bracket. Time then is the most expensive or valuable of all. Do you agree?

Time is precious. Have you heard that before? So, if time is precious and you are one that does not value time and is not intentional about time, excuse me to say that you cannot achieve success. I say this because you need time to read, meditate, speak, sleep, work, and act on all that has been spoken about previously in this book.

Time is the ultimate thing and it is freely given but it does not last forever. And that is why I want to take a minute to talk about how to manage it effectively. After all, this book is about knowing what you should spend your time doing.

The first thing I want you to say out loud and have probably not told yourself before is this:

I have a time limit!

Lots of people want to live forever and am not talking about an eternity in heaven. They even fear death, even those that say they have a hope of heaven. The rich pay so much to stay young and invest in unprecedented and limited medicine just to ensure they stay alive, but the truth is, we all have a time limit.

With that knowledge in mind, let's start thinking about how to make the most of the time we have.

Time audit

The starting point must be correcting your perception of time. Some people think they have the whole time in the world, whilst others are so scared that time is going, that they are demoralised by it and do little to nothing about it.

Do an audit. Create a log of what you do with your time. I know some apps can do this for you. The time you spend flipping through Facebook pictures, Instagram posts, following an advert that pops up on your phone, watching series on Netflix. I am equally guilty of this, especially after a major win. However, I am entitled to know exactly how much time I spend on all this activity and weigh the value of the activities to me.

Pleasure is equally important in life, but it must not take over my passion and the value I add to others. This is my legacy and my gift to the world. A true legacy is an impact you make on others that lives on when you are gone. Ten years, a hundred years after you, living on in your children, followers, and mentees.

So, take stock of your time and know where the bulk of your time is spent. This is the only time you should be looking back at time. When you are reminiscing over the good times and evaluating what and how you have used your time, maximising it to bring about a better future. No regrets, just lessons learnt, and accolades gathered.

One such time is when you gather friends and family to celebrate you, you would be surprised at what you have achieved, the lasting impressions you have left with people. Would I have some regrets? Certainly, but learn from them and focus on the positives, it's more beneficial that way.

Do you know you probably are the most critic of yourself? This is because you know the little details about yourself that others don't know.

Some of these details didn't get past the thought process before you uprooted them and acted right, but you keep imagining that people can see all of that. Never mind, remember those self-affirmations, we talked about earlier? Use them to correct your mindset when these thoughts come to flood your mind, refuse to let it sweep you off and take charge over your mind once more.

Time heals all things when you use the aspirin of 'self-affirmation' in the right dosage to keep your mind in check and stay positive minded and healthy.

Birthdays

This is an opportunity for an audit. At least for me it always is. This year I had a zoom party, never thought there was any such thing, but 2020 brought out certain things and some disruptive initiatives that we never thought about before the pandemic. So, I had friends from all over the globe in one place, talking about 'Moi'.

People I cared about and cared about me too, saying what I desperately needed to hear, 'Victoria, you're doing great'. Were they lying to me? Maybe? But I chose to believe it all. Believe that these kind words, expressions of my deep thoughts were seen, experienced, felt and received by real people. I was influencing more people than I thought. Whether you are living intentionally or not, you are influencing someone, now I encourage you to spend more time being intentional about the story you want your life to paint. The history you leave behind and the gift the world has just because you are here.

If you are reading this, I believe you are alive! I'm laughing right now. You are alive because you still have something to give. When people are done giving that's when they give up on life. So, start thinking of how and what solution you want to bring the world.

Time/ task management

Set a time limit to the tasks you carry out. It helps prevent procrastination and unproductivity. It also gives you a satisfying sense of fulfilment and accolade.

High achievers know how to account for every minute of their day. Even if you have excess time because you are on a holiday, your whole life isn't on a holiday. The only time your whole life can be on a holiday is when you have put the right amount of work in and are now reaping the reward of it.

So, start with that to-do list and make sure it has a time limit to it.

Here's an example of a to-do list.

6:00 - 6:30 Devotion Meditation Prayer

6:30 - 7:30 Write

7:30 - 8:30 Self-care and breakfast

9:00 -10:00 Study and research topic

10:00- 11:00 Shopping

11:00-11:30 Call Friend/ check social media

11:30-12:30 Lunch/ unwind/ meditate

12:30 - 1:30 Attend strategy meeting

2:00 - 3:00 Marketing

3:00 -4:00 Teatime

4:00 -5:00 Assignment

5:00 -7:00 Dinner/ family time

7:00 -8:00 Read

8:00 -9:00 Bible study

9:00 Bedtime

This is just a sample and is by no means a fixed routine.

A to-do a list like this will help you tick off what you have been able to achieve in your day and what was left undone. This can be added to the next day's to-do list and note, appointments and future engagements should be uploaded into this list as they come to avoid double-booking your time.

You can make this as formal or informal as is required by you. You also need to know your passion must be reflected in your daily activities. It is the summation of all your little activities daily. Without a plan, you waffle through your day doing trivial duties, never really achieving anything, that is the biggest thief of time.

It becomes a little life game.

Have you heard of RPM- Result, Purpose, and Massive Action?

A to-do list can end up being a list of should dos that never get done; it does not possess the emotional leverage needed to get it done.

RPM provides that leverage by attaching actions to a purpose. Start with the PURPOSE, it can be 'being my own boss'

Then you put next to it a RESULT 'being a 'healthy hair coach who provides alternative styling solutions'

Write down the 'key ACTIONs to get there.

A good RPM will have a 6-12 months action plan attached to a result which in turn results in a larger purpose. - Putting the why before the how- benefits dependency framework.

Physicist Richard Feynman said 'the first principle is that you must not fool yourself and you are the easiest person to fool'

Now, in terms of investing time in this book. It will help make giant leaps in your mental leaps because you cannot stockpile, buyback, or make more of it. So, time spent building yourself, learning and growing is time well spent.

Get a taste of your potential and be excited at the results your making because of it. Get comfortable being uncomfortable!

Mornings

I am in awe of the morning sounds from the birds that coo to the silence of the trees. The movement of the invisible wind to the brightening of day and the darkness fades away uncontrollably to give the stage to the dawning of the day. This seamless transition is beautiful to watch when I get the privilege to, as I am not an early riser, but I am becoming somewhat of a morning writer. I hear the different sounds of the birds, so distinct yet different all in their arrays as they fly into and out of the big tree in my garden. It is in my neighbour's garden, but it overarches mine.

I sometimes play the game of guess the bird, but I have not been good at naming them. So, I just enjoy them and distinctively hear six different cooings. Right there in my little garden. I wonder how many more kinds are out there in the vast world.

Oftentimes, I stand like the trees in the summer morning, and watch the light shine through the crevices of the leaves of this huge tree, just like the stars sparkling the dark sky with its light. It forces its way through to illuminate my garden as the sun rises from the east to the west, the leaves getting a dose of their nutrients as it allows the flood of light through, ensuring it gets the best of the array of light for its food.

Your mornings are the most important, along with everything it brings. A fresh beginning and a ray of hope almost unstoppable that ushers you into the next reality of your dreams. Another day, another opportunity to use time. Do not let it slip by without getting the dose of your nutrients, utilities of the seconds and minutes, as you glide upon it and ride on it leading you to a brighter tomorrow, the one you have so often had a glimpse of on a day you allow yourself be taken away by your dreams and swept off your feet by the flood of thoughts in your mind of what may be. Unknown to you the power of your will and the energy it exerts to empower you for executing those plans, so deeply buried in your thoughts.

Start early and start with the 'Must Dos'. Mark Twain, an American entrepreneur and author, once said *'If it's your business to eat one frog, you should eat it first thing in the morning, and if it's your business to eat two frogs, it's best to eat the biggest one first'*.

Say no

You cannot answer everyone's question or solve the world's problem, especially not this morning, if you are to answer the call to accomplish the big questions and overcome the elephant in the room. What you can and should do is spend your time answering the question you are built to solve, the relevant and difficult one you are trying to push back, using your morning strategically to ensure that.

So, SAYING NO does not mean you are cruel. Perhaps you could answer more people more effectively if you answer your one question that will serve a million people who have been waiting for it.

'The morning time is the crux of the day' a Yoruba adage says - Yoruba, is a tribe in Nigeria, mostly spoken in the southern parts. **'If you waste your morning you will work twice as hard to recover your day.'** The morning which has an equal time of your day as your afternoon has its energy that makes difficult tasks surmountable.

In other words, do the biggest, most pressing, impossible, and daunting tasks first. Utilising your energy in this way can be a boost for the rest of the day. The sense of fulfilment can be the drive for the rest of your day whilst your most challenging tasks have been tucked under your belt, leaving you with a grin and a sense of accomplishment that might as well last you the rest of the day.

Ever heard the statement 'got off the wrong side of the bed?'

How you start influences what you do for the rest of your day and how well.

The Afternoon

This time might be less attractive, popular or the stunner. It has its dazzle. Fast-paced, buzzing and filled with people and activities. Perhaps over cramped with activities that could have been achieved in the morning, now dumped on it with over-expectation and ambition. You are being less energised but pushing harder to keep the momentum going in other to fulfil the set tasks. It is a time to take deep breaths, cos you will need it, use your energy wisely, making sure you only exert it where necessary, the afternoon drags long, unlike the dash of the morning.

Delegate

It is as important as completing tasks yourself. Delegation is a skill that many refuse to master but it is a way of leveraging your afternoon or morning perhaps.

Wanting to accomplish everything but in doing that accomplishing nothing is the story of so many that refuse to learn this simple and humbling skill. It is a way of leveraging your time and doubling your efforts to have quantifiable results. So, outsource if you can afford it, take the offer for help, or pass on some simple tasks to your subordinates, let them shine too. You will be leveraging your time and mastering your expertise. It is a way to make the most of your afternoon and the company will help the long drag of the day pass quicker too.

The Evening

Just as its name implies, is neutral, as you begin to balance the equations in your mind. Have I done enough? How well have I answered the questions of today? Which tasks are left that cannot be put off till tomorrow? All the questions start flooding in like the rush of wind on an oceanfront. Calm it down and control those thoughts, do not allow it to overwhelm you as can be the norm for this time of day.

You are not perfect

Only God is perfect! Yes, I said it. We all aspire to perfection and continue to do so, but no one is perfect, so perfectionists spend a lot of time on one task hoping for it to be perfect and in the end, you find someone else has done it better than you did. The truth of the matter is that, you have your audience, you are enough, and you will have different versions of yourself, an update perhaps every year or so. Knowledge is not stagnant. Do not be scared to decimate the version you have produced and then work on it as you go. So be realistic with the time set on a task, do it to the best of your ability, and move on from it. The evening is 'welcoming in', an end to the day, you should too.

The will

Your Will is an aspect of your mind. It is often pressured by external factors in a way that it underestimates, suppresses, and thinks of it as not relevant.

Will is the answer. Lots of people might 'Will' for you to be successful like I do for you. I have spent so much time writing this book and coming this far, but the only Will that matters is yours, so you 'Will' it for yourself.

I will become an author

I will make millions writing

I will influence my generation

I will help people find their purpose

I will and now I am becoming what I will for myself and so will you.

The process is part of it. Pay attention to your will. Utilise all that has been said to quiet the noise of your mind, so you can hear your will, that is where the power lies. In your will.

Your will as a driving force

Will is a powerful force. Have you seen a young person who has a belief to follow a part? He/she will abandon a course, the people known for years, just to follow a part that he/she is convinced about. Or when you hear a nice motivator, like Les Brown, one of my favourites, teach on goal actualisation. You come out and you believe you can and then you begin to pursue it.

Expectation shows up in behaviour, not the things you talk about or claim but in what you are doing. When the shouting has died down and you decide to go to university, you decide to invest in yourself, or you read a book. Please note again that money will not make you happy, but everyone is trying to find out for himself.

Money should not control you, You should see it as a tool that helps you to live a life of contribution to the lives you have been waiting to influence,

Money gains friendship. Even the people who do not like you will find something nice to say to you.

Establishing a project to pursue your dream. Be willing to do the things today others will not do in other to have the things tomorrow others will not have. Discipline must be a major character. 1 % of the 1% understand this.

Anything worth doing is worth doing right but if you don't know how to do it right, ensure you get doing it so that you can get better at doing it and getting it right.

Do not stop doing it when you don't feel like it because you will never find out you could do it if you never gave yourself the chance to do it. Even when people laugh at you don't let it bother you. You just *keep moving* because you will eventually get better.

Face that fear

Life begins at 40! Really!

As my birthday approached, the 37th year I couldn't help thinking. 'Wow, where did the time go?

Just a minute ago I was 17, feeling young with my life ahead of me with an almost too certain optimism that I will be a millionaire by the time I am 40. And now am 37 and 'I cannot see the hundred thousands rolling in yet. Did I do something wrong? How did the time go so quickly?' And then I remembered this phrase. 'Oh, that's what it is, a consolation that I shouldn't give up yet because those earlier years are going to go so fast, I'd be running to keep grasp of it so it doesn't leave me behind.'

Firstly, if you are younger than me, and you are reading this book, don't worry so much about the future, things will fall in place, but remember all my big sisterly advice…. Use it, you will thank me later. If you are a peer and are in this age bracket, *life begins at 40,* grinning. You have done what you have, pat yourself on the back for it, it's almost afternoon, identify what has been holding you back if you're not where you want to be and are not yet spending enough time on answering the big questions. Also, face the fear and start taking the hardest papers now. Don't leave it till the afternoon, you might not have enough time to complete it.

Lastly, you might be much older than me, most likely *wiser*, you might or might not be answering the questions yet, but like the evening time, draw an equilibrium and assess the ups and downs, you are bound to have had, you've been around long enough to have enjoyed living in that way. Take the lessons, leverage your time, and only spend your time on the important questions, rest is nigh.

Face that fear, because it is going to keep coming back until you stand up to it and face it. Use everything within you to fight back. When life throws you a lemon, make lemonade they say. Lemonades are my favourite drink!

Despite that fear, *act*, it is not real. It is a facade. The minute you walk through it, you would ask yourself why you waited so long. Do you know everyone experiences fear? Even the people you see and think 'wow, they are so confident, I wish I am like that'. They have fears too. The only difference is they do not communicate their fears, they only speak their confidence. Like I say to my daughter, 'say what you know not what you don't. Stop telling yourself I *don't know* because there are a thousand other things that you do know, talk about those.'

In other words, when you focus on what you do know, and you affirm that to yourself by talking about it, you grow in confidence, deeming the spotlights on your fears and relegating it to a mere shadow and a negligible reality, even if it is real.

Growing in confidence in this way will lead to you to mastering that talent and becoming aware of your weapon for facing your fears. Everyone has a weapon. For some it's word, others writing. It could also be intelligence and many other skills that you can identify in yourself or as others pick it up in you before you do. Just make sure you are developing it and using it to its full potential to empower you.

Knowledge

Knowledge they say is power. Knowledge is about getting to know what is right and what is good, well that is the starting point. Knowledge of a subject area can equip you with influence, money, and a platform. It is a starting point, the means to an end.

What do you know? What can you say boldly that you know? This friend is the starting point of your purpose. The things you know, and give your time to know, direct the course of your life. So my decision to know God as a teenager redirected the course of my life so adversely and directed me in a way that I did what was required at the right time because, a bigger force than I am, with a wider view than I do, was telling me how to go. I am not saying I always followed it rightly, remember I have a will so whether or not I aligned that to God's will determines my action. Knowledge or the lack of it guides our decision. So, if you find that you are not being decisive about your goals, get some knowledge about it, in no time you would be heading in the right direction.

Commitment

Your habits reveal your commitment. Be honest with yourself and analyse what you spend your time on. Spend your time on the ideologies you believe in, the things you do relentlessly and tirelessly, things you will do over and over again without gain, Now commit to them, improve it and make it it into a product or service.

When I committed to my degree at Middlesex University, I made up my mind I was not going to quit halfway. I also decided then to pay for my tuition rather than take the student loan. Guess what, I did pay it off, I didn't say it was easy, I had to do quite some extra work, developed my hairstyling skills in that season, and was fully committed to the course. That means, I did whatever was possible to do, things that were ethical and within my belief to do and came out with no debt. Stop! You have your own stories and they are a part of your journey. Do them, so you can live to tell them and inspire whoever wishes to listen.

So, commitment is doing whatever it will take to get the result you desire. Have you heard the story of the egg and bacon? The chicken was involved but the pig was committed. I am laughing again. Yes, he had to give all to be part of that dish. So, give the commitment of the pig rather than the involvement of the chicken, it just is not enough.

Talent/ Skill

Start with that. If some of you will only give half the commitment you give to completing an assignment, an academic paper or a being a football fan or even trying to fit into a friendship circle you don't even belong to anyway, you might already have been a millionaire by now. Or is it the amount of time you spend scrolling through people's stories on Tik Tok, Facebook and Instagram combined (these are social media platforms that is ravaging our time in this 21st century) some reading this book might not get it. These are just trends, be involved but do not let this be your commitment.

Your talents and skills are where you should be spending more of your time. Developing your speaking skills, practising your basketball, your piano, and those other skills apparent or that a good friend is constantly nagging about. Stars are not born! They are made out of habitual practice and dedication.

Faith to act on what you believe in

You are going to have to summon the courage from within. But this faith to act is a catch-22. The action shows your faith and the faith is required to act. Do what you can per-time and not focus too much on the big picture. Start from the small little habits you do daily.

Faith in yourself and ability to act on that desire is everything, until then no one knows what you are made of and you will be living a borrowed life. It is not enough to exist, you were born to live, make it meaningful, make it worth it.

Money

I would not have spoken about money here if I had my way, but I must do. Money, they say, makes the world go round. But I say 'Money answers all things'. It gives you the platform to stand, an opportunity to influence and help the world with those things you so desperately want to change.

My favourite book says a man that has money has many friends. Even your worst enemy will find something nice to say to your face.

Money is the means to actualise your dreams, it is going to fuel your birthing it. So, it is important to know how to get wealth. Whether it is a job or a business that brings you money, find a way to master, allocate and maximise your income.

I am no expert on this topic, but there are lots of writing on managing money. Have you heard of the 70%/10%/10%/10% rule? Well, it goes something like this. Once your income comes in, spend the first 10. The next 10% should be allocated to TITHE, GIVING, CHARITY. Another 10% to SAVINGS/INVESTMENT, another to PLEASURE. The big 70% goes for BILLS AND NECESSITIES (debts, utilities, etc.)

However, this ratio will need to change as your projects get bigger, but this is a good place to start. What then happens if your 70% cannot cover your necessities? It means you have to put to practice all that we have talked about in this book so far to leverage your time to build your second or third stream of income.

Now elating money with happiness. Can money buy happiness? I have been in want and have had more than I need, and in both seasons, I can say it's the thoughts of the mind that prevails. I have seen a man who has it all yet seeks more, and another man who has little but so great content so much so that he exhumes more joy and happiness. I have therefore concluded that being happy is a choice we make. A decision that you and I need to make to ensure we live a life without constant regrets.

Money will get you lots of things but ultimately, it's your choice to be satisfied by it or not. All the money you have will flow according to your mindset. Money has a link with your thoughts, actions and results and it can control one's life. The abundance or lack of it has a way of influencing one's life. However, a person can grow and mature into a state of happiness and contentment irrespective of the amount of money acquired. It is with this state of mind that a person can be more productive and get more out of life. Being empowered over one's emotions is the goal, being congruent with it, and having clarity on who you are and where you are heading. Not losing this clarity is a lifelong process that you must continue to invest in and provide yourself with. I guess that leaves us the question, how do I maintain the momentum. That will be a topic for my next book.

However, not all value can be quantified in money.

This last chapter is addressed to a believer of Jesus Christ!

As a fellow brother or sister. I address you this way because you have a wealth of provision at your disposal in Christ Jesus. Ephesians 1:9-10

Can I intrigue you with this thought that God knew from the beginning that man would fall but that did not stop Him? Rather he made provision at the right time, in Christ Jesus, that we might be predestined in his will and perfected through the Holy Spirit.

You have a WILL POWER! This power is stronger than your fears, failures because it has all been paid for in Christ Jesus. You have a bigger force rooting for you, one that has overcome all things and given you the power to live a life of fulfilment.

Can you begin to see what God has for you?

It is all complete in Him. Renew your mind and know who you are and who God calls you. Only then can you receive this restoration he has given you.

The works of restoration. According to the Greek word 'apokatastatasis' means to bring back into former position; to produce anew.'

That is to a better position than Adam was. Where we have the full maturity of Christ, 'the second Adam'.in a position of total Victory, just like our saviour is. Matching onto the enemy's territory and taking what is rightfully ours, with a fully restored position of total control over every aspect of our mind and thoughts, where you know what to do per time, a knowledge of your purpose and your position in the army of God, to be a blessing and a good ambassador and representation of God on earth.

Spend time in the word of life. Like the psalmist says, 'your word have I kept in my heart that I might not sin against you'. The word is thy mirror for the life you are seeking. It tells you all that you are and where you should go or what you should do.

Joshua 1:8

It tells you to wake up early to praise him,
Spend time to meditate day and night,
To speak the words- prayer,
Then you will have good success.

These principles the father has left for us in His word so we would not be confused, so go on and win the battle in your mind and tell yourself these.

I know what to do

I am doing it and seeing results

Things are working out for me

I am an overcomer

I follow my will!

Go and be a winner doing the things you know to do.

The end.

Notes

Printed in Poland
by Amazon Fulfillment
Poland Sp. z o.o., Wrocław